from my
soul to yours

e.russell

leaf
publishing
house

for amy
thank you
always

i spill my soul word by word in
hope to help fill yours too

contents

you

————————————⟲

keep watering yourself
you're growing

you gaze upon
the stars so often
you have forgotten
how bright it is
you shine yourself

without
waiting
to be
saved
you
saved
yourself

life is too precious
to share yourself
with those who do not
wish to be kind

this earth
knew it
needed you

now you do too

they say
beauty is in the eye
of the beholder
but your beauty
could not be held
for it is found
within your heart

these tears
will not
run forever
darling

these tears
will run dry

they say
beauty is in the eye
of the beholder
but your beauty
could not be held
for it is found
within your heart

these tears
will not
run forever
darling

these tears
will run dry

be your own muse

you must
first find
happiness
within
for you
to then find
happiness
in that
of others

self acceptance

do all
with love
as love
will do all
for you

they
will still
have love
for you
when you
believe not

to know
what it is
to rise
you must know
what it is
to fall

so fall
graciously
but rise
ferosciously

you are still here
fighting to this day
and that in itself
is more than enough

just to be you
what a privilege that is

better
yourself
for
yourself

it is easy to believe
that you are not enough
but you cannot even comprehend
how enough you actually are

no matter the struggle
you are here now darling

you will not know
love for another
if you do not know
love for yourself

you cannot
grow
planting
yourself
in darkness

if you
do not
bleed
out the
bad
how
will the
good
ever
return?

purge

to be you
is a gift to existence
in itself

it is ok
to not always
feel like
the best version
of yoursellf
so that when
you do
you will feel it
more significantly
and that
significicance
can only ever grow

only settle
for those
who make
you
a better
you

do
as your
heart
tells

listen to it always

ethereal
and pure
you glow
a sight
of pure
enchantment
too precious
for a
world so
unsightly